Fields of Fire

STEVEN LESLIE HILL

An environmentally friendly book printed and bound in England by
www.printondemand-worldwide.com

Mixed Sources
Product group from well-managed
forests, and other controlled sources
www.fsc.org Cert no. TT-COC-002641
© 1996 Forest Stewardship Council

FSC

PEFC Certified
This product is
from sustainably
managed forests
and controlled
sources

PEFC
PEFC/16-33-415
www.pefc.org

This book is made entirely of chain-of-custody materials

i

www.fast-print.net/store.php

Fields of Fire
Copyright © Steven Leslie Hill 2015

The right of Steven Leslie Hill to be identified as the author of this
work has been asserted by him in accordance with the Copyright,
Design and Patents Act 1988 and any subsequent amendments thereto.

A catalogue record for this book is available from the British Library

ISBN 978-178456-222-9

First published 2015 by
FASTPRINT PUBLISHING
Peterborough, England

Best Wishes

Oliver Leslie Steel

This book is dedicated
to the memory
of
Zbigniew Gwardzinski
(Gee)
1950 – 2014

One of the Royal British Legion and life's finest gentlemen

Acknowledgements

I would sincerely like to thank the following people who have helped make this book possible.

Lee Chapman
Cover design, layout and artwork.

Tony Higton
Internal photographs, WW1 expert knowledge and valued friendship

Susan Hill
Typing, page layout, proof reading, love and support

Fast-Print Publishing
All printing and publishing

Introduction

O ne hundred years ago, the guns finally fell silent on the Western Front after over four years of trench warfare.

The conflict claimed in excess of 37 million casualties of which over half that number died on the battlefields, and millions of the survivors were mentally and physically scarred forever.

After the conflict ended, many more soldiers committed suicide due to their traumatic experiences. Also the total of casualties does not include the civilian population who lost not only family members, but also their homes and all their worldly possessions.

Many events and individuals during that brutal war will be remembered, in particular:

The Christmas truce of 1914, the taking of Vimy Ridge by the Canadians, the slaughter on the first day of the Somme, the shear horror of Passchendaele, the executions of rebellious French soldiers at Verdun, the horror of gas warfare and the bravery and chivalry of Baron Von Richthofen and Albert Ball are just a minor few that come to mind.

Millions of soldiers, nurses and civilians carried out acts of incredible bravery and self-sacrifice of which only a handful were ever adequately rewarded.

As with my previous books on this subject, I have tried to capture through poetry and verse the terrible waste of human life and man's inhumanity to his fellow man, but also the love, humility, comradeship and courage of those who gave their lives for freedom.

I hope you enjoy my final personal salute to them all.

Steven Leslie Hill

Fields of Fire
Somme Battlefield
Present Day

Fields of Fire
Forever red
Once covered in blood
Now poppies instead

Thousands upon thousands
Cover this ground
In memory of the Soldiers
Who were never found

Standing tall
All as one
Just like the men
Who died on the Somme

And as seasons pass
With generations of old
May the courage of the fallen
Be forever told

For their names will live on
Long after we are gone
These Soldiers of the Great War
Now ghosts of the Somme

Goodwill to All Men

Christmas Eve 1914
German Soldier

Snowflakes slowly fall
And cover the frozen ground
All along the front line
There is silence, no sound

For tonight, no machine gun chatter
Or constant cannon boom
Just soft snowflakes falling
Underneath a bright full moon

This is Christmas Eve
A night without fear
A time for reflection
And thoughts of ones so dear

Children around the world
Are happy Santa will arrive
While we here in the trenches
Are just happy to survive

And they can all sleep soundly
In a nice warm bed
While here in Flanders Fields
We sleep with the frozen dead

And on this night of merriment
Of joy for old and young
When Christians come together
And Christmas carols are sung

A night of good wishes to all men
To keep fear and hatred from our door
And I know the wish out here on both sides
Is just simply, no more war

Life after Life
Loos Battlefield
France 1915

Is there life after life?
I guess there must be
A place where the soul
Can finally be free

And if there is a heaven
Then there must be a hell
And the latter is a place
I know very well

For hell is here
On Loos killing fields
A place where 'The Reaper'
Cuts all his deals

And I wonder what our creator thinks
Looking down from on high
As we destroy the earth
And blacken the sky

Killing each other
Without a moments pause
All for greed
And some political cause

No respect for the living
Or for the dead
Just mindless destruction
From an empty head

And like sheep to the slaughter
As the blind lead the blind
To a place where sorrow
Is all that we find

And how much more misery
And pain can we take
Before we realise
That war's a mistake

And instead of this greed
Death, sorrow and strife
Why can't we all just live
This one precious life?

Neuve Chapelle

France
1915

Five minutes to go
I give the order down the line
My men wait with bayonets fixed
Marking this precious time

Five minutes
That's all that's left in life
Oh how I wish, dear lord
I could once more see my wife

I look at the men around me
In their thoughts, they all look lost
For in the next five minutes
We all know what this day will cost

Then suddenly the time is past
'Up and over', my whistle blows
Who, if any of us, will survive this day
The answer, God only knows

Dedicated to the memory of
Lieutenant Colonel George Brenton Laurie
1ˢᵗ Battalion Royal Irish Rifles
Who led the assault on the German positions and was
subsequently killed in action

Rendezvous with Death (Part One)

French Soldier
On Route to Verdun 1916

I look at your face
As in Paris, I board the train
And my love I pray I will live
To see you and the children once again

For yours is the heart
I hold so dear
But I have a strange feeling
A terrible fear

That this will be
Our last goodbye
And at Verdun
I am destined to die

And in that place
I will take my final breath
For I have a rendezvous
A date with death

Rendezvous with Death
(Part Two)
French War Widow
1916

I am sure he is here
I feel him sometimes
A reassuring presence
That everything is fine

It was at Verdun
Where he lost his life
Three years after
I became his wife

They say he was a hero
On that terrible day
And the loss of his own life
Was the price to pay

But I know he still watches
Over our children and me
And I'm sure he's at peace
And his spirit's now free

For he was my hero
The rock in our lives
And until the end of time
I will always be thankful
He chose me as his wife

Devil's Wood (Delville Wood)
France 1916
South African Infantry

I was muscle
I was bone
Now I'm a soul
So far from home

I once felt love
I once felt pain
Now I know nothing
Will be the same again

I walk in darkness
I walk in light
In this wood
Through the bloodiest fight

I see death
I see war
I see friends
Who exist no more

I gave my flesh
I gave my blood
I gave my life
In the Devil's Wood

Dedicated to the South African Infantry who fought with great
courage in the Devil's Wood

Toy Gun
British Soldier

I remember as a child
I played with a gun
It was a toy back then
And we just played for fun

Now I am a soldier
And still carry a gun
But this one's for real
And no longer for fun

For the bullets they hurt
And the pain you feel
Nothing can prepare you
When you kill for real

It's then when you wish
Your gun was still a toy
And you were just still
That happy little boy

Butterfly
German Soldier
Verdun, France

It danced in the morning sun
Above the shell holes in 'no man's land'
And as it came closer to his trench
He gently stretched out his hand

It landed on the mud
Flexing its wings in the sunlight
An angelic vision of beauty
Such a rare and colourful sight

He slowly raised himself upwards
Forgetting the danger and fear
That's when he made
The French sniper's target clear

A single rifle shot
Echoed across 'no man's land'
And as he slumped forward dead
The butterfly gently caressed his hand

Inspired by the original 1930's German film "All Quiet On The Western Front"

The Spirit

I was with you
When you took your first breath
And I will be there
At the time of your death

For I am your spirit
Your guide, your light
And will keep you safe
In the darkest night

I am the truth
That will conquer the lie
For I can turn darkness
Into a clear blue sky

I am your soul
Who's with you each day
And I find the answer
When you kneel down and pray

And when you are broken
And losing the fight
Then forever believe in me
Your spirit, your soul, your light

'Albert'

British Soldier
Albert, France

He doesn't look much
This old terrier I stopped to feed
But we have grown to care for each other
So very much indeed

He trotted along beside me
As we walked the ruins of Albert town
And in each other a comfort
We seem to have somehow found

We eat and sleep together
And fight the Germans too
But if I lost old 'Albert'
I don't know what I would do

And if God willing
I see this war to its bitter end
I hope I can return to England
With my little canine friend

For I would dearly love to see him
Roaming free on my Dad's farm
Away from all this misery
Where he will come to no harm

"So watch out Fritz"
Because me and Albert are back in the front line
And if you want a bloody nose
We will give it to you every time"

Dedicated to all the thousands of stray and homeless dogs who provided companionship, and were mascots to many regiments on the battlefields of France and Belgium.

Battlefield Tank

Deadly withering fire
From mortar, shot and shell
It rolls through it all
Like a beast from hell

Its machine gun opens up
With bursts of fire
As it smashes on through
Their defensive wire

Cutting men down
Forward, left and right
Destruction and death
By dawns early light

The battlefields now littered
With the dying and the dead
As the rain soaked mud
Turns 'blood' red

Then a shell explosion
Blows the tank on its side
A burning metal coffin
For the men inside

Another day of slaughter
In the 'war to end all war'
Dear God, please tell me
What the hell it's all for?

Fragrance of A Rose
(A Poem from the Trenches)

Like the fragrance of a rose
Warmed by the summer sun
You brighten my life
With your beauty and love

And when I see you smile
And feel your touch
I know, my darling
Why I love you so much

To see you laugh
With your soul full of life
I know I am lucky
To have you as my wife

And when this war is over
And all the killing is done
Hand in hand we will walk again
And feel the warmth of the summer sun

Home Thoughts

I want to go home
That's a simple fact
Preferably with all
My body intact

To my home town
My favourite place
Where I can have a drink
With a friendly face

No more corpses
Lice and fleas
Where the only smell
Is a warm sea breeze

To walk along the cliff tops
Just Hannah and me
With a spring in my step
And my mind so free

To kiss my Mother
And shake Dad's hand
To be home again
Oh, so grand

A nice warm bed
Instead of this trench
Away from the rats
Mud and stench

But first we've got to do
This job here in hand
Before we can leave
This war torn land

So I guess I'll soldier on
Until I cross 'the foam'
So prepare a good reception
When the boys come marching home

The Cruel Sea

The cruel sea awaits
Unforgiving and stark
Her waves roll with anger
So cold and dark

In sub-zero temperatures
And freezing rain
We cross the vast ocean
Of the Atlantic once again

And in the deepest depths
Of its murk and mire
The submarines await
To unleash their fire

A cat and mouse game
That has only one end
Where any mistake
Is the grim reapers friend

Tossed and turned
Battered and worn
Hoping each night
Will bring a new dawn

On this ocean rests the fate
Of our ship and me
For death awaits us all
In this dark cruel sea

A Place in England

There is a place in England
Somewhere I would like to be
Where a coastline so rugged
Meets the wild North Sea

The mist rolling in
As the breakers crash the beach
Standing on the headland
It's so clear, but so out of reach

For I now lie here
As my life it ebbs away
Mortally wounded on a foreign field
So many miles away

And as the cloak of death
Takes me from this place
I can almost feel the sea mist
Its wetness on my face

For England, my England
Oh how I love thee
Please God take me back
And let my soul be free

But if I am to walk the darkness
I know I won't walk alone
For we are the fallen soldiers
Who never went home

Life Taken
British Soldier
The Somme

I look at the face
Of the life I have just taken
And wonder who he was
Did he have a family the same as me?
And in his death
Is his soul now free

Or will he walk forever
In a cold, dark place
Trying to find life's door
And when I die
Will I see him once more?

And if I do meet him
What would I say?
For "sorry" seems not enough
To have taken his life
This way

For war is brutal
Survival in its extreme
Oh how I wish
This day would end
And that it was just all a dream

Glass Eye
British Soldier

Through a glass eye
The telescope of my gun
I watch my target
In the morning sun

For the night time ghosts
Return me to that place
And the glass eyes cross hairs
Always frame his young face

I squeeze the trigger
And in a second he is gone
But the image of his face
Forever lives on

For there are wounds that are physical
While others touch the mind
And these thoughts of the past
I always somehow find

And each night they are here
As wounds that won't heal
Caused by war
And hot lead wrapped in steel

Bollocks and Bull
Australian Soldier

To hell with all the Generals
And other Officers too
Cos if you ask us 'Cobbers'
The 'bastards' aint got a clue

And as far as the Sergeants
With their fancy three stripes
Barking 'bloody' orders
All day and night

Just a bunch of 'arseholes'
Full of 'bollocks and bull'
Who's mission in life it seems
Is to make our 'bloody' lives dull

Practising for this
Marching for that
Running around
Like some thick, headless 'twat'

So if I survive
This 'bloody'war
I aint never gonna take
'Bollocks and bull' no more

The soldiers of the Australian and New Zealand forces (ANZACS) were some of the toughest troops and fought in most of the conflicts with great distinction and honour, but who were not renowned for their love of Officers and 'Top Brass'

War
All Nations Soldiers

Do politicians really care?
When they send us all
To God knows where

They tell us we are fighting
For a noble cause
But it seems like to me
That war breeds wars

You kill one man
Then you face ten more
Escalating the cycle
Of hate once more

And when all the bloodshed
And killing is done
And you look around at what
War has done

The broken bodies
Misery and pain
But you can bet the politicians
Will have you do it again

It seems to me
For them wars just a game
But for us on the front line
War is insane

Revenge

French Soldier
Marne 1918

I hate 'Le Bosch'
Despise them all
This is my chance now
To even the score

For my comrades and friends
I have lost
For my nation that's paid
Such a cost

To rid my country
Of the German 'swine'
Be rid of these pigs
For all time

No quarter given
No mercy shown
Just send them all
To 'hell', their home

And make France
Free at last
For today's the day
We all avenge the past

Dedicated to the French Infantry who fought with tremendous courage and bravery in defence of their homeland and in the cause of freedom

Cross in the Mud

British Soldier
Ypres Area

Shell holes and craters
In a landscape of mud
Full of stagnant water
Corpses and blood

Up on the horizon
When you cast your eye
Some fire charred trees
Still reach for the sky

And across in the distance
Ypres old town stands
Now just rubble
On this war torn land

Canadians to our left
Anzacs to our right
Bayonets fixed
Ready for the fight

And as the Officers whistle
Sounds down the line
For some of us today
Will be our last time

Will heaven be ready
To take some more souls
Or is there just nothing
Nobody knows

No rest for the wicked
No peace for the brave
Just a cross in the mud
Above a deep, dark grave

Sleep My Brother
Belgium Soldier
Dicksmunde

Mud wall trenches
Steel sheets and barbed wire
All across our land
That's been scorched with fire

Twisted stumps
Of lifeless trees
The smell of death
Carries on the breeze

And this morning at dawn
Was my friend's last stand
Before he was killed
On this ravaged land

So sleep my brother
Deep and well
For you no more
Of this war torn hell

Dedicated to the 93,000 Belgium soldiers who gave their lives in the 'Trenches of Death' in defence of their homeland

Where Angels Fear

Being a British soldier
Means simply being the best
Each time you hold that gun
Your training is put to the test

Fighting in this hell hole
Where angels fear to tread
We will keep you safe back home
In your night time bed

And the daily freedom
You all cherish so dear
Is because of the deeds we do
In this place of pain and fear

We ask only one thing
Pray for our safe return
So we can have that time with our loved ones
We have fought so hard to earn

Dark Corners of the Mind
United States Soldier

I volunteered for 'Uncle Sam'
And did my time
Now I am back home again
And working the local mine

But what I witnessed there
Was a terrible spilling of men's blood
Where men's lives were taken
In the filth and mud

I changed my miner's shovel
For a helmet and gun
And somehow I survived
Until my time was done

But I can never forget
The horrors I have seen
As now they live as pictures
Forever in my dreams

The memories of that time
From the dark corners of my mind
Take me to a place
Where I'm back on the front line

For it seems I must return
To that land I know so well
Where again I walk upon
The burning fields of hell

Silent Guns

11/11/1918
United States Soldier

They will never see the light
Of a day's new dawn
Or hear the cry
Of a new life born

Never again see their families
Or America, they loved so dear
Their last moments on earth
Were consumed in fear

My brothers in arms
The courageous and the brave
Their only reward
Is a deep, cold grave

A cross for a pillow
The earth for a bed
The final resting place
For America's fallen dead

*Dedicated to the Infantry of the United States of America whose
bravery and courage helped secure victory for the Allied Forces*

Peace for Everyone

Across 'no mans land'
A snipers shot is loud and clear
And another mother somewhere
Will cry and shed a tear

For her son who has been taken
While far too young
When will all this misery, lord
Be finally over and done

For as the years move on
And over a century has now passed
Wars and conflicts they still rage on
And it seems they are here to last

Peace for everyone
It would be nice, but don't hold your breath
For history has already shown us
Mankind's love affair with death

Band of Brothers

The valiant fallen
From all corners of the globe
They all died young
So will never grow old

And shoulder to shoulder
Together as one
We brothers pay our respects
From Verdun to the Somme

For their spirits will burn always
And their memory will never die
For they dwell forever in glory
In God's kingdom upon high

Brief Goodbye

Life's journey never really ends
And our spirits, they never die
Just onward up the road
To that ether in the sky

Where we will meet again
The friends and family from long ago
In that place of eternal peace
Where love is all we will know

For life's journey never really ends
And our spirits, they never die
For this moment here in time
Is but a brief goodbye

Maple Leaf Soldiers

Canadian Infantry Monument
Belgium Present Day

He stands eternal
A sentry made of stone
Guarding his fallen comrades
Who fell so far from home

Head bowed in respect
Rifle in hand
A monument to sacrifice
In a foreign land

Vimy Ridge, Passchendaele
Ypres and the Somme
They died in the cause of freedom
Heroes, everyone

The fallen Maple Leaf Soldiers
Like autumn in the fall
This monument and its soldier
Will forever guard them all

*Inspired by the monument at Vancouver Corner in Belgium and
dedicated to the Canadian soldiers who gave their lives*

Britain's Fallen

Present Day
Great Britain

Through every town and village
Across every field and plain
There will be a monument
Inscribed with their names

Great Britain's fallen heroes
Who fought for a better world
Forever now remembered
When our nation's flags unfurled

A reminder of these brave souls
Who died guarding freedoms door
A sacrifice for liberty
In the war to end all wars

*Dedicated to the British and Irish soldiers whose sacrifice in the
name of freedom must never be forgotten*

Ghosts of Flanders Fields
Present Day
Belgium

Thousands of poppies
Among fields of corn
The sun warms the earth
On a brand new dawn

And in these fields
A century ago
Battered by the elements
Of rain and snow

Young men died
And were never found
Do their restless spirits
Still walk this ground?

And when I look now
Over Flanders Fields
I think of what
This land conceals

The shells and the bullets
Flesh and bone
And the ghosts of the dead
Who never went home